Return to Fuller Street

Return to Fuller Street

Beverly Tucker

ILLUSTRATED BY BRUCE MACDONALD

MARINER
PUBLISHING

IN ASSOCIATION WITH THE
HISTORIC LEXINGTON FOUNDATION

Copyright © 2020 by Beverly Tucker

All rights reserved, including the right of reproduction in whole or in part in any form without the express written permission of the publisher.

1 3 5 7 9 10 8 6 4 2

Library of Congress Control Number: 2020900687

Return to Fuller Street
Beverly Tucker

p. cm.
1. African American History
2. Virginia History

I. Tucker, Beverly 1938— II. Title.

ISBN 13: 978-0-9992885-8-0 (softcover : alk. paper)

Cover art by Bruce Macdonald
Edited by Judy Rogers
Book Layout by Karen Bowen

Mariner Publishing
131 West 21st Street
Buena Vista, VA 24416
Tel: 540-264-0021
www.marinermedia.com

Printed in association with
Historic Lexington Foundation

Printed in the United States of America

This book is printed on acid-free paper meeting the requirements of the American Standard for Permanence of Paper for Printed Library Materials.

*Proceeds from this book support
Historic Lexington Foundation's programs and publications.*

This book is dedicated to Metz, Tuney, and Tick
who inspired me as a child

and

to Rosa Wiggins
who inspired me as an adult

Table of Contents

Acknowledgments ix

Introduction xi

Chapter 1: Metz 1

Chapter 2: Marylin Francine Evans Alexander 9

Chapter 3: Brenda Woodley Miller 19

Chapter 4: Wendell Holloway Baker Jr. &
             Priscilla Nowlin Baker 29

Chapter 5: Lucy Evans Ferrebee 39

Chapter 6: Margaret Joyce Henderson Wright 49

Chapter 7: Maria Elizabeth McLellan Quillin 57

Chapter 8: Irene Elizabeth Pennick Thompson 65

Chapter 9: Vaden Hamilton Thompson Jr. 73

Chapter 10: Leon Harvey 79

Chapter 11: Tuney and Tick 87

Epilogue 89

Acknowledgments

The House on Fuller Street was inspired by the Historic Lexington Foundation's (HLF) purchase of a house at 205 Fuller Street in the Diamond Hill/Green Hill neighborhood in Lexington, Virginia. Following the Civil War, Heyden and Rebecca Holmes—an African American couple—purchased the property, then expanded it during the next twenty years. The Holmeses came to be greatly admired in Lexington. Upon their deaths, they were buried in Evergreen Cemetery, the city's African American cemetery.

In 2010, the City of Lexington posted plans to demolish the house on Fuller Street. HLF purchased the property and stabilized and restored the exterior. Getting acquainted with the neighbors on Fuller Street encouraged a series of oral histories, which morphed into HLF mounting an exhibit at the Campbell House with the cooperation and support of the Rockbridge Historical Society. The exhibit, entitled "A Dialogue with Diamond Hill," was a great success and would lay the groundwork for a book, *The House on Fuller Street*. A part of that series of events was a panel in which alumni of Lylburn Downing—the traditionally all-black school in Lexington—returned to speak about growing up in Lexington during segregation and integration. Support from the Historic Lexington Foundation and the Rockbridge Historical Society was vital in these projects, which would likely not have occurred without it.

It is the author's hope that we honor these individuals and that we learn through their stories about the lives of African Americans in Lexington during a difficult and trying period in our nation's history. These individuals grew up before and during integration and experienced first-hand the changes wrought by the Civil Rights movement, Equal Opportunity, and Affirmative Action. Through their oral histories, we learn of their experiences, feelings, and opinions. When asked about progress, most expressed the feeling that much ground had been gained but there was still much further to go. Still, one must admire their positive attitudes throughout and their strong sense of community. It could be said that a question answered by Metz in the first book received affirmation in the second work and will serve to take them through whatever lies ahead.

Since the publication of *The House on Fuller Street*, we have lost many of those people featured. We are indeed fortunate to have their stories in the published interviews. This book adds to the ongoing story of a resourceful people who deserve to be long remembered.

I wish to thank Rosa Wiggins, Marylin Alexander, Irene Thompson, Don Hasfurther, Dr. Spencer Tucker, Bruce Macdonald, Suzanne Barksdale Rice, and the entire Board of the Historic Lexington Foundation as well as the Rockbridge Historical Society. It has been my privilege to become acquainted with the individuals featured in the profiles. My hope is that on reading their accounts, you will feel the same bond.

Beverly Tucker
2019

Introduction

For those of you who have read *The House on Fuller Street,* you will soon be reacquainted with the main characters of that book. You will also remember that the first book was a story in which the fictitious characters, who live in a fictitious house, were used as a mechanism to introduce the true oral histories of real people in Lexington, Virginia.

You met Metz, Tuney, and Tick, three generations in an African American family. Metz, the matriarch and grandmother of the story, is not only mindful of their family's past history, but is focused on questions concerning the future as it relates to her people. She is a leader in her family and community and sets a personal goal of attempting to understand the significant repercussions for her people who were literally kidnapped and brought to this country against their will. She hopes to unravel the perplexing question of what it is that seems to so profoundly bond these individuals to each other, always keeping a part of who they are within themselves. That same underlying question presented in the first book is continued and reaffirmed by the protagonist here in the second.

This book offers an important glimpse into the lives of people who have lived through difficult times to survive, and in some cases thrive, as a consequence of having discovered their

value and their **values**. These are stories that will remain with us long after these special people are gone.

"*Return to Fuller Street* is a wonderful collection of accounts and stories that centers on life in the African-American culture in the city of Lexington, VA. The common thread that binds these chapters together is the love among the family that is expressed all throughout this literary work. Dr. Tucker methodically illuminates these citizens of this Western Virginia locale to a radiance that is far brighter than one can imagine. The First Baptist Church is the centerpiece of the African-American life in Lexington. Fuller Street is no exception. Through the church programs and mission work, it is not surprising that those who read this book will comprehend the marvelous influence that the First Baptist Church yields to the community. All of the chapters contained multiple levels of interest that a family or an individual would appreciate and enjoy."
— The Reverend McKinley A. Williams, Pastor
First Baptist Church of Lexington, VA

"And all the memories of all we have loved,
 stay and come back to us in the evening of our life.
 It is well to treasure them."

—*Vincent Van Gogh*

Chapter 1

Metz

    The reassurance provided by the early morning sunrise was just what was needed by all who lived in the old house on Fuller Street. It was, of course, good to know that the sun would still come up. But the familiar footsteps and the perks of the coffee pot were silent. It was nearly impossible to count the times in the past that Metz had been the first one down to see that the day had a good beginning for Tuney and Tick. The two employed women would hurriedly join her before repairing to their respective daily endeavors of earning a living.

    That same sun gave a welcoming shimmer through the window above the sink and created a bright spot on the old green linoleum on the kitchen floor. It was a welcome expression from Mother Nature, and it would have been typical of Metz to say a little prayer of thanks. This old house had been good for this family, standing the test of time, limited funds, and years of wear, along with lots of love.

    Firmly built on that most familiar Fuller Street, it was one of the larger houses, for it even had a second level. The stairs were worn and would likely stay that way as the smoothed edges bore witness to the many steps that had been taken there. Metz had often said that she wished she did not need to climb those steps to her attic room but reasoned that it was good for her knees and back and so declined a move to the lower level. It was a good thing she was not tall because the door to her room was quite small. She loved that room.

Even with her trifocals, her eyes had given up much of her sight, but still she had carefully learned to sense her way up those stairs, an arthritic hand carefully placed on the railing. Metz's parents had managed to buy the place, and though it still carried a mortgage, it had been passed along to her. After many years, it was finally hers. When her husband, Thomas, died, Tuney and Tick came to live with Metz there.

Over time, and after retirement from domestic help jobs, Metz's days had evolved into a fairly simple set of tasks. There was always the cleaning and laundry, church on Sunday, trips to the river whenever all could get together, summer gardening, and autumn canning when the garden bounty was harvested. That bounty had been shared with others, and she was known for her famous chicken hash, which she especially prepared for funerals. This year there would be no bounty, no canning, and no chicken hash, for the ground stood barren.

Tuney was nearing retirement from the drudgery of housekeeping, and for Tick, well she walked across the stage to receive a college degree and was now employed in social work for the Commonwealth of Virginia. To her, that cap and gown had been the most beautiful dress she had ever worn. Her daughters, Milauna and Kawana, had done as so many other young people in Lexington had chosen to do. They left. They had made their way to cities where work was more likely to be found. Milauna worked at a gift shop in Maryland and took part-time courses at the junior college. Kawana had enrolled in a four-year college and was working in the cafeteria to make ends meet. She had been awarded a scholarship and hoped to become a nurse. The family had relatives in Maryland, and this was close enough to home without being too close.

With the younger ones gone, the three generations of women who had lived together happily had continued to do so. There in the house on Fuller Street, there was always a leaky roof, a cracked window, or a room that needed to be painted. Repairs were eventually accomplished when they had the money to pay for them. Once they painted the front of the house, then saved their money and several months later had the back done also. Thus their pride of place was always reaffirmed.

There was Metz, the matriarch, who had become the guardian of the trove of rich memories of their ancestors. Tuney had been left alone to raise her own little daughter, Tick. The devotion of this generational triumvirate was expressed daily with love, work, and mutual support however needed. Even during Tick's predictably awkward teen years, her mother and grandmother rallied around her and they made it through that precarious time without severe repercussions. No drugs, no breaking of the law, no reckless driving (of course at that time there had been no car).

Though not the storybook form of family, the three women were happy and never took for granted their good fortune of relative security and comfort. They had compensated for the loss of the men in their lives and learned the lessons of necessity. They could do what needed to be done. In each of them there was still some of that notable ancestor, the one who picked the cotton. It was Metz who kept that piece of the past alive in them and would not allow them to forget. It was also Metz that had reflected on the hard questions throughout her lifetime. She recalled the impression left on her by a long ago evening of a gathering of African American people who had grown up during the difficult years of *The Green Book*, that flimsy little thing that listed acceptable places where they would not be turned away because of the color of their skin. They recalled life in the times of segregation, integration, and equal opportunity. They remembered that they were not allowed to finish high school in Lexington but had to go away for the last three years.

Metz knew the speakers, invited as a panel, who could articulate the years when they had grown up in this small town with the two colleges. This was a town where gentility reigned, but those of color lived in a certain area and went to a separate school where their football team wore hand-me-down uniforms donated by the colleges, and even found humor in never knowing what their school colors would be in a given year. They had tattered used books purchased at the school book depository, later to become a pool hall, then much later a restaurant called the Red Hen.

So it was on a stormy evening all those years ago that a crowd had gathered at their Lylburn Downing School to hear a panel discuss their experience of growing up as black children in a Virginia town. Those who attended reported it to have been a fine presentation. Accounts heard that evening agreed that it had been a good place to grow up. Each speaker recalled their experience filled with anecdotes ever so positive, harmonious, and sometimes humorous.

But there was an elephant in that room...a great big issue that hunkered down hoping to be answered. There was no mention of *The Green Book* or the tattered books, or the lack of test tubes in the chemistry lab. There was no one who mentioned having to go away to high school in order to graduate. Then as people departed, one small woman spoke quietly, almost to herself.

"We didn't tell it all," she said. "We didn't tell it."

Thus, Metz had taken these questions as her own. What did the people on the panel really feel? What did they hold back? Why did they not speak their true feelings? With comments carefully guarded, most knew that much had been avoided. The elephant was still in the room.

It was Metz who stayed the course in her personal quest to consider that question, and throughout her life she sought the truth, desiring only to understand. Her tired body supported her keen mind. One evening, as she sat in the kitchen simply engaged in sewing on a button, she reached her own profound conclusion. It was this grandmother with the dark skin and the white hair that, to her own satisfaction, offered an answer that made sense.

It was not a sudden epiphany. It was based on reading, listening, and observing until she felt emotionally prepared to give shape to this jarring proclamation to herself. Metz reasoned and wisely concluded...that there was a certain place that the black community could go within themselves to reveal their feelings, and that those feelings had been formed in the belly of a ship crossing the middle passage from Africa.

Those who were living in the present might have listened and heard her thesis and although not physically chained to that ship, still felt the anguish of this experience that had reached across the years and had become their own painful bond. To withhold some aspect of that journey to themselves was a way to stay united. It became a personal burden that only they could understand. These chains were physical, mental, and emotional, even at a time some of these dark-skinned people were being tentatively invited into the larger culture. That invitation was tentative and unreliable. For Metz, to understand this and to finally put it in words, made it okay. It was the invisible bond, now accessible to those descendants who had not made that cramped and cruel forced journey across the great expanse of ocean.

Some limited progress had been made—there was even the election of an African American president. Metz's regret and sadness was clearly about the progress that was yet to be realized. She was sure she would not be here long enough to see it through. And with certainty, there would be vacillation on the part of all involved and what appeared to be forward steps were soon questioned as the nation grappled with answers. But Metz was getting old, and she was tired, and much of what had to be done would not be accomplished in her lifetime.

Metz's departure from this life was unexpected and had been hard for those left behind. She had remained alert until she was taken ill, and the process of her dying was brief. In her faith, she was reassured that she would join Thomas, who had died so many years before. She had really loved Thomas, and part of her had gone with him.

Her death, of course, brought friends and relatives together to honor her life. A service at the church was followed by a large number of the congregants gathered for a picnic at the river. This had always been one of her favorite things to do, and her wish for this had been expressed to her family many times. The choir was mightily rehearsed after many years of these outdoor gatherings and the harmonic strains of "Amazing Grace" made sparkling ripples on the great North River now known as the Maury. Then all was quiet.

For Tuney and Tick the void was huge and the house on Fuller Street felt solemn and empty. Metz had been their rock, their ever present inspiration, and now, save for the powerful memory of her strength, they were on their own. Their grief left them paralyzed. There was an emotional turbulence within, and they put off the things that needed to be done. They were reticent and shy, hesitant to enter her room, that sweet place always so bright and happy as she had long ago painted it a deep red, her favorite color. The years had left their mark on the walls, but to her it just added to its integrity and charm. In the past, they had gone there many times with an expressed need for her counsel. For these two, who had been so connected to her, the challenge of going through Metz's things and deciding what to do accordingly, was a chore they put aside for months.

By the time they finally launched that task, their findings made hesitation seem foolish. There was much to do and decisions to be made, but somehow those came naturally as if guided by her presence. They arranged her clothes to be taken to the church for others to use. Each took a sweater and a robe that they could wear and feel her warmth. They savored this time as it provided some easing of the pain.

Well into the first days of their work, they found in the back of her closet an old army trunk, which had belonged to Thomas when he had served in the army infantry. With due respect, they sheepishly approached the trunk as if it was sacred and were overwhelmed with what was revealed. Carefully making their way through the delicate layers, in the recesses of that dilapidated trunk was a lifetime of records including diaries, a marriage license, a picture of Thomas, and a tattered ivory dress with a bit of lace and beautiful buttons. A corsage so fragile it could not be touched or identified was securely placed in a small box with a date of some seventy-five years earlier. At the bottom of the old trunk lay a thick book with yellowed pages, handwritten records of people Metz had known, admired, and loved.

At one time, the color of the book had been a dark rich blue with gold clips. Now a faded lilac, it was a frayed legacy—the threadbare gift Metz left behind. These were the recordings of her life as it was observed and put on paper in her labored handwriting. It was titled "People I Have Known, Their Grace and Meaning to My Life," a long title but one carefully considered. Carefully turning the aging pages, Tuney and Tick realized the full significance of their discovery. The recorded profiles of the people in Metz's life lay bare those pieces of living that she valued most. It appeared that she had spent hours listening to and recording the stories of these people, who worked hard, lived by a strong faith, and knew the true value of friendship. She was a good listener.

Tuney and Tick sat down for the first of many visits to read this extraordinary collection of tributes. They came to view those intimate looks into these lives as a time to be with Metz and a time to remember.

Chapter 2

Marylin Francine Evans Alexander

Metz's Note

I remember so clearly the days I visited my friend Marylin, who I admire more each day. Her life has stood out and is well above the ordinary. She distinguished herself with her dignity and served as a model for an effective life well lived.

Marylin

My birth date is July 19, 1953, and we just celebrated my sixty-sixth birthday for almost a whole week! I was born at the Stonewall Jackson Hospital on Washington Street. It was down in the basement where other black mothers had their babies. Dr. Pleasants was my mother's doctor, but he was black and not allowed to practice there, so Dr. Munger assisted my mother in that delivery. He signed my birth certificate.

I was the last of four children, and my sister Wynona was ten years older and still the closest in age. I think I was a surprise. The oldest was my brother, George Evans Jr., known to us as "Skip." Then came my three sisters—Sissy, Elizabeth, and Wynona.

Marylin Francine Evans Alexander

My name, Marylin Francine, came from the names of my mother Mary and my father's sister Frances. Those names are very dear to me. My aunt, Irma Thompson, helped name me and all the rest of my siblings. She is very special and is now 102 years old, still living in Buena Vista.

We grew up at number 11 Massie Street to be exact, in what was known as the Green Hill neighborhood. It was a white stucco house with a screened porch. It was a house full of family and love, with children in and out all the time. My mother was wonderful and the best cook ever. My siblings' friends were all older, but they loved to come to our house. My parents welcomed them, and mother always had something for everybody and of course plenty of food.

My Aunt Kitty (Norma Thompson Murchison) also lived on Fuller Street, and half of my time I was at her house. She was a teacher in Glasgow and Buena Vista, and thus much of my "early learning" was with Aunt Kitty. She would take me to the library, and we would get ten or twenty books at a time. I would take them home and devour them immediately.

My mother was a beautician. Both she and Aunt Kitty gave me a great deal of attention, probably too much because I was spoiled rotten, or so that is the story I am told. I didn't want to go to school and begged to stay at home. I thought I had the best of all possible arrangements, and I cried every day for the first two years of school. It finally got better.

My siblings grew up and left home for college or military service. I was essentially raised as an only child, which I thought was just fine. I attended Alice Moore Nursery School. I was in the very first class there and also one of its first graduates. I have always been very proud of that. I then attended Lylburn

Downing through the seventh grade all during segregation. Then it was integrated during my eighth grade year. They didn't have room for us at the high school, so we stayed one more year at Lylburn Downing. After eighth grade, we went to the high school in Lexington, from which I graduated.

It was always taken for granted that all of us kids would go to college. It was not a matter of when—it was a matter of where. When I look back on it, I can't help wondering how on earth my parents were able to provide for college, our clothes, our related expenses on what they earned. But they found it somehow, and we all went. My sister got a part-time job working at the Sigma Alpha Epsilon fraternity house.

My father worked at the cannery and at VMI, and I recall him telling a story that I will share with you later.

My brother went to Bluefield College and then into the military. One sister went to Virginia State University where I visited her often for football games, programs, and homecomings. I ended up going there too, and we both graduated from that university.

After college, I got married. We wanted a family and never did I think that would be so difficult. I had so many miscarriages that we finally decided to turn to adoption. We got a baby girl and named her Mallory. But there were some rough moments, and ultimately my marriage ended, and I set out to raise my little girl alone. We lived in the house that I grew up in and still live in now.

I was very satisfied with that arrangement. I was not interested in getting married again and didn't date. But sometimes fate has different ideas as to what is in store for us. Some years later, I went with a friend to hear an outdoor concert in Lexington. The band was called Karisma, and its lead keyboard player, Rick Alexander, was a friend I had known in elementary school. I recognized my friend, and apparently he also saw me and was determined to make a connection.

Thus started a barrage of phone calls, drive-bys, flirting, and attempts to get a date. For some time, I resisted all efforts. Finally, he did manage some calls, and from August until October, there were many conversations over the phone.

One afternoon, I was outside at home with Mallory, and lo and behold, Mr. Rick Alexander came to call. With his long hair and mod clothes, he looked much like Michael Jackson. Mallory excitedly exclaimed, "Momma, Michael Jackson is here!"

Rick and I were married in 1992. In spite of fertility issues, our daughter Michelle was born in April 1994. The months I had to stay in bed were well worth the results of her arrival. Her premature birth resulted in some health issues that still surface today, but she is not impaired by them. In fact, she is strong and happy.

At that time, I was still working, and the job I found myself doing was a reminder of my father's story, the one that still hurts when I think about it. During the years that my parents were sending so many to college, my dad was working two jobs to help the situation financially. He worked at the cannery and at VMI, but when he got laid off at the cannery, he had to attempt to qualify for unemployment benefits. I was very young at that time, but I remember him telling the story of his trip to the Virginia Employment Commission.

The room was crowded, and he was the only African American there. He took his number and began what became a day-long endless wait because they would not call his number until all the white people had been served. He waited and waited until everyone else was gone. He was finally called. That story has stayed with me throughout my entire life and will be forever. I was so hurt to hear how he had been treated.

The irony of this story is what took place many years later when I had the opportunity to set things right. After college, I decided to take the exam that is given by the state for all state jobs. I had majored in sociology and later took the licensing exam for becoming a social worker in the state of Virginia. Of all places that I might be assigned, I was to work at the very office where my father had been treated so shabbily. I vowed that all would be treated equally and that would be done in the order which they had arrived rather than the color of their skin. I was there for twenty years, so I had many opportunities to make sure that fairness was a part of that operation. After all that time, things changed and I recognized the need to make and seek new challenges.

I became involved in Human Resources and ultimately went to work for Target. I was their recruiter for filling the jobs required for a new operation. Over time, my work took me from town to town, Staunton, Buena Vista, and Fishersville. Our daughters had reached an age when they needed a parent in town, so I decided to leave that position and work in Lexington.

My family had some connections to the Mountain View Terrace Apartments, and I was considering managing them—all forty of them. My dad said, "Don't get involved in that—it is hard." But I did it anyway, and often I think of his words of warning and now know what he meant. However, I have been doing it for twenty years, and there are some days in which I think of what my father said. He would be pleased to know that I would confirm his opinion and advice.

There was a flexibility to that job, and one good thing it did was allow me to get back into being involved in the community, to serve on the school board and then the city council.

As I think back over my life, beautiful and meaningful memories come to the surface. I recall with joy the wonderful childhood, the wonderful neighborhood, the characters, the friendships sustained throughout my lifetime. We had so much fun with the simple things. We played! We skated, rode our bikes, we had a seesaw, and when it snowed, we had sleds making run after run down those hills so familiar and so accessible. I also remember the reassurance of a mother who had her beauty shop in the back of our property so that we knew she was there and always available to our needs. I remember going to the White Front Grocery with my parents.

I learned many lessons in those early years and not all of them were easy in their message. One significant memory took place at Christmas. I was always so excited and could believe I actually heard Santa's reindeer on the top of our house. Having heard that magic, I decided to make my way down the stairs to see what had been left for me. I played with all the toys, and in my excitement, decided to go ahead and open all the packages marked to be mine. I was up most of that night, but close to morning, I slipped back upstairs and into my bed.

Of course, in a short time, all the family was up and on their way downstairs. They were having so much fun and laughter as they opened their gifts and enjoyed what Santa had left, but I had nothing—for me it was all over and had been for several hours. I felt terrible! I vowed then and there that I would never ever do that again. I remembered that lesson and throughout my life stuck with the vow I made. I had learned the lesson of pleasure from delayed gratification and the unpleasant results of breaking the rules, even if they were informal but understood.

My mother never gave up on believing in Santa, and even as adults, she would admonish us with: "If you don't believe, you will not receive; if you do believe, you will be rewarded." Those wise words could be applied to many aspects of one's life.

In my own adult home, we have tried to provide a safe place where our children can see the importance of education and experiences that show us a larger world. We wanted exposure for them to such things as music, art, and integrity. We even built a pool at our home so that they could have their friends over and we knew they were all secure. We tried to set an example and provide answers to their questions.

We sometimes encountered meanness and statements from others such as, "You act white, and you ain't white." Such rubbish must be dismissed with the hope that ultimately humanity will win.

One of the most significant memories of my life was the election of Barack Obama as president of the United States of America! An African American in the most prestigious office in the world! And at that time, I was making my first run for City Council of Lexington, Virginia. I was on the same ballot with Obama, and I could not believe it! I was not sure that I would win and hoped above all things that Obama would win. We both did! And that was one of the most glorious memories in my lifetime!

It might surprise you but I had to really push myself to be comfortable in these public roles. I am an introvert by nature, and because of the requirements of the office, it took a great effort on my part to become a public official. But those years are the best. I grew immeasurably and in the process hoped to have made some difference here in this community.

Because of some health issues, I will not seek a third term on the City Council. I am excited that my cousin is considering a run for my seat, and I go on record as saying that she would be excellent in that office. There are still many things that I can and will do as a citizen.

I am troubled by the upheaval in our nation. Some of the rhetoric one hears is so mean and so divisive that it has the sound of words and deeds witnessed before the American Civil War. Now when people spew their hate, especially those I thought I knew, I am dismayed and fearful of what lies ahead. I am also realizing that we have been cut into pieces.

We have to stand tall and resist hate as if this disarray has never happened. If we give in to fear and cower to it, we make it possible for it to take us over. We cannot bend to hate and bigotry. As Elijah Cummings said, "Let us reclaim the soul of our nation." May he and we all eventually rest in peace.

> "There are ghosts of yourself scattered everywhere. Whispers of a moment suspended in time where every life that you have brushed up against, now lives with a piece of you trapped in your mind."
> —Erin Hanson

Chapter 3

Brenda Woodley Miller

Metz's Note

Finding where Brenda Miller lived was not easy. She had given directions to her home, and it sounded easy enough but actually getting there was a challenge. She had given the apartment number as "Building C." Well, the "C" was missing on that building, and frankly they all looked alike.

Finally I found the right place, and she did not hesitate to share her memories.

Brenda

I was born October 29, 1942, the daughter of Patsy Ross Hamilton, in Clifton Forge, Virginia. I can't recall if I was born in a hospital or at home. I think it was more likely at home because that is how it was mostly done in those days. I remember very little of Clifton Forge because we moved to Lexington when I was very young.

I lived with my grandmother, Jessie Morison Woodley. We called her Minah. She taught school for forty years. She taught me in the first, second, and fourth grades. At first we lived on Ruff Lane until we moved to Massie Street. I was baptized in the First Baptist Church when I was six years old, and that church has had me in it for every year since. That church means so much to me and my life.

I had two sisters and two brothers. They lived with my mother. One of my sisters is deceased, but my still-living sister, Jessica, is in Washington, DC, where she retired last year. I am proud to tell you she worked for the Department of Commerce at the time of her retirement. Earlier, she went to Georgia to teach. Then she came back to Lexington and enrolled in the Washington and Lee Law School. She did well in her studies and in her profession.

My mother lived up on Brushy Hill and was married to a man named Berkley Hamilton. He was a character if there ever was one. He was always doing something crazy. He went across the country on a wagon train. He did a lot of plowing for people in the area. Let me tell you that man was a character, bless him.

I don't remember so much about when I was real little, but I remember going to the church and making homemade ice cream. I don't think my family had many traditions, for example at Christmas time, we got one gift, maybe a toy, a piece of clothing, some candy, and fruit. And we really appreciated what we got. Children don't seem to appreciate things so much anymore because they get gifts all year round.

At Christmas time, the church always had something for us, maybe some fruit or some candy, but the highlight was doing the Christmas plays…and the music. We would sing and the women of the church made our choir robes. I remember Virginia Brown and Eloise Johnson. Those women were wonderful. Miss

Brenda Woodley Miller

Alice Moore would train us. I remember Lucille Croft. She was a wonderful cook, and she was so generous and caring to teach me to cook and let me bake in her stove. She let me come to her house, and we would have just the best of times in the kitchen cooking.

I still love to cook and will be making a cake for church this Sunday. I like most of all when we have our soul food dinners. I have cooked pigs' feet for those dinners, and one lady who ate some said they were really good. You cook them by boiling them, but the secret is in the seasoning. The boiling alone won't get it! I also love to cook for the Black History Month event. And I love to make cornbread! I even love my own cornbread, and I remember one time when I baked several pans of it, took it to the church, and planned to have some myself, but in the blink of an eye, it was gone and I didn't get any of it. I just made some more.

One of the best memories I have was watching western movies in the basement of the church. We would watch those movies on Saturday nights, and I thought it was wonderful.

At that time, some very special entertainers came to perform at Virginia Military Institute and at Washington and Lee. I am talking about big names like Count Basie, Duke Ellington, and Dizzy Gillespie. My grandmother knew the lady who provided housing for all the special entertainers that came to Washington and Lee. There were certain places that they could stay and other places where they could not, so private homes or those designated in *The Green Book* were favored.

My grandfather worked there, and he would take me to see Basie, Ellington, Gillespie, and other big entertainers. It was pretty exciting to slip in and hear that great music. Afterward, they would often move the band over to the Knights of Pythias building, and they would continue well into the night. There was a big room with plenty of room to dance, and the bands would come over and play for free. Those were exciting times, and looking at the old K of P building, I long for those days. Virginia Military Institute did move and save that building because of its historical story, and I have heard that it will be a part of the new building being built on that spot. I'm glad it was not destroyed because of its meaning to the black community here in Lexington.

I love music. Music is my thing, and my greatest regret in my life is not continuing my education and studying music. I would have loved to be a singer or a choir director. I will always regret not having done more with my education and with music.

My grandmother made me take piano lessons. I hated being inside practicing when I could hear all the kids outside playing while I was inside at the piano. I would say, "Here I am, got to be practicing when I want to be outside." I realize now what an opportunity that was, and I let it go by. Why can't we know the things we need to know when we need to know them? By the time we learn, it is often too late.

I went to Lylburn Downing High School. Fortunately, when I was there, we were allowed to finish there, whereas before the students had to go away to finish the last two years. My mother went to Christiansburg to finish high school. I was lucky that things had changed by then somewhat. I never felt the heat of segregation. We had white neighbors on Massie, and we all played together and we were friends. At least for me I did not feel anything negative. It never bothered me, and the only time anything unpleasant happened was when our teacher took us to

North Carolina on a trip. We couldn't find a place that would let us in to eat. I know now that there was a little book that would have given us some guidance about where to go, but we had never heard of *The Green Book*, which was supposedly a guide to tell black people where they could stay or eat safely. I learned about it later. Now I suppose it is no longer needed.

My grandparents loved to fish and would go as often as they could. I really didn't have a choice about whether or not I would go, but I admit I did not enjoy fishing. So I would take a book, some ginger snaps, and some cheese and sit on the riverside and read. I sort of liked putting the worms on the hook, but I had no interest in catching a fish.

After high school, I got married to Alfonzo Miller and started having babies. I had three boys, Cabot, Bucky, and Darin. My husband had a garage called Round Hill Garage out on Route 11. He was also a mechanic at Washington and Lee. My son Cabot worked there too later, same job. Bucky worked there too until he later became an officer on the Lexington Police force. He is well known and liked in the community, serving in a variety of ways. Even now he helps out at a summer camp.

Of the three boys, Bucky seems to be the only one that is healthy. The other two and I have a serious kidney disease. At one time, we were all three on dialysis at the same time. Cabot has had two kidney transplants, and Darin has always been very sick. He has been away for the last nine months in a nursing home. He is back with me now, but he is still sick. It seems to be hereditary as my mother had it too. Cabot just had his second transplant. He was working on my car when they called and said, "We have a kidney." Of course when they make a call like that, you have to drop everything and get there.

Bucky took his brother on Tuesday, but they didn't do it, so he took him back on Thursday and the procedure was completed. The first transplant didn't work, but we are hopeful that this will be better. I get up at 3:30 a.m. to get my other son, Darin, off to dialysis, and then I go the next day. I used to have a day to rest, but now there is no "rest day." Now every day is scheduled for one of us.

I still drive my car. Something was wrong with it, and a man took $1,000 from us to fix it, and it wasn't fixed. I am waiting to get it back. I am thinking of writing to the Better Business Bureau and reporting what happened. I am not sure it would do any good, but it is wrong to take money for a service you don't provide.

I was asked recently, since I had three boys (there is so much stereotyping of black males), if I had done anything to prepare them to behave in a way that would protect them from being taken advantage of. Did I worry? Yes, there is worry, but the two oldest ones had a strong father and a model to go by. They knew there were things they just weren't going to be able to do. The youngest lost that father when he was three. So he always looked up to Cabot more as a father figure. They are all close. There were times of trouble, but by and large they are fine, and I am grateful for them.

I have many grandchildren and great-grandchildren. Some I don't get to see very often. Some once in a while. Some live in Staunton, so the chances of my seeing them are better, but I would still like it to be more often than it is. Everyone is so busy these days.

I try to make this place as pleasant as I can. I like African American art and posters. That one over there has the words of former President Barack Obama on it with his picture. I am very proud of that president, and I miss him. There is a little table there that was my grandmother's, and I am so happy that I am able to have it and to keep it in the family. I have threatened to haunt my three boys if they don't take care to keep it after I am gone.

I have been in this apartment for two years. I had to move to this smaller one. I have been in this apartment complex for seventeen years, but I moved to this place on the ground floor so that Darin would not have to climb the stairs. But, not having room, I had to give away many of my things. That was really hard to do, but you do what you have to do, and I had to do this for him. He lives here now. He'll be coming through that door any minute now. He has been for a treatment. It is strange that we are all sick with the same problem.

My home is not federal housing. In fact it is privately owned by someone who pays very little attention to the needs of the tenants. The owners of this property are not here very much, and when things go wrong, it is hard to find someone to fix whatever is broken. My bathtub is built up on a high platform for some reason, and it is nearly impossible for me to get in it, but I really have no choice.

You may have noticed that it took me a while to answer the door. My wheelchair has a hard time making it through all the furniture that is double stacked for lack of room. I am sorry you had to wait. I try to keep a good attitude. I have that television on just to keep me company at times. My son Darin will be back from his dialysis treatment any time now.

As you can tell, I have been in Lexington a long, long time, and I remember so many people. Right now, I still remember all their names but am not sure how long that will last. My memory is pretty good, but my mind jumps around from one thing to another. There have been many wonderful people who had an influence on my life.

The person I most admire is Michelle Obama. I would really love to read her book. I hear from many that it is a wonderful book and so is she. I was so proud when President Obama was elected.

My fondest memories are all related to the First Baptist Church. I love the picnics, the dinners, the singing, our fellowship, and the times we have been together. I miss so many of those who are gone. Oh so many are gone.

> "You never really understand a person until you can consider their point of view, that is until you climb in their skin and walk around in it."
> —*Atticus to Scout in* To Kill A Mockingbird

Author's Note

Several weeks after this visit, Brenda's son Darin died of kidney disease. Though she was greatly saddened by this, she acknowledged that he had suffered enough and had gone to peace.

Also, Brenda Miller served honorably as the Sister in charge of the First Baptist Church's 152nd Anniversary Celebration on September 15, 2019. She is still working for the church.

Chapter 4
Wendell Holloway Baker Jr. & Priscilla Nowlin Baker

Metz's Note

Wendell and Priscilla represent all that is good and right in this world. Wendell worked more than fifty years as a barber, and Priscilla was a registered nurse. Their stories can be held up to any and all. Wendell and Priscilla are two of my favorite people individually and even more so in combination as a couple. They are more or less "institutions" in this community. Praise be that I had the good fortune to know them.

Wendell

I was born in 1937 in Lexington at the Stonewall Jackson Hospital. As with many other African American babies, my mother was confined to give birth in the basement rather than upstairs with the white mothers. My parents were Marie Baker and Wendell Baker Sr., who also had three other children, Marylin, Hortense, and Deborah. I was the only boy with three sisters.

Wendell Holloway Baker Jr.

After a happy and rather ordinary early childhood, I went with my family to Philadelphia where my dad had work. Then we came back to Lexington where I was enrolled in school at Lylburn Downing. That was a good school. I remember some of the teachers: Miss Jessie, Miss Nelly, and several others. Those were good people. It was there that I played football and got really interested in music.

After graduating from Lylburn Downing, I was accepted to attend the University of Toledo in Ohio where I majored in physical education. One of the highlights of my life was to be a part of a band called The Rhythm Makers in Lexington. I played the saxophone and we traveled all over the place. We were popular with the white community as well as the African American, so we never lacked for a place to play. Our lead singer was an amazing person. He didn't have any arms, but he not only could sing, he could throw a baseball with his feet. Everyone admired his talent and determination.

One of the most exciting things that related to my love of music was the opportunity to hear the professional bands. Count Basie and Duke Ellington were just two of the greats who would come to Lexington to play for special events at W&L and VMI.

One time when Duke Ellington came to town, after the program was over, he came over to the home of Priscilla's aunt. She had a piano, not a very good one at all, but he sat down and played that piano, and it never sounded so great.

After I graduated from the University of Toledo, I went to Washington, DC, to barber school. I was there for sixteen months and was lucky to be able to stay with my cousins. I went back to Lexington and went to work for Dave Moore as a barber in the lobby of the Robert E. Lee Hotel where I stayed for the next ten years.

After those ten years, I opened my own shop on Jefferson Street, and there I stayed for almost fifty years. On my days off, I went over to VMI to cut the hair of the cadets. I also had many friends at Washington and Lee, and often alums would return for a visit and always come get their hair cut. It was interesting to me to see that the white people came to our barber shop, but the black community went to the Franklin Barber Shop where Ted DeLaney's grandfather and his aunts and mother were all barbers.

Once a W&L graduate came into the shop and he said, "Is Wendell here?"

I said, "I'm Wendell."

He said, "No I mean the one that cuts hair."

I said, "That's me."

He said, "You are still here?"

He couldn't believe it. They respected me, and many alumni would bring in their sons to meet me.

I was a sometimes "counselor," and I would let them know that I could be trusted. I would never repeat those things that were told to me. One day a man came in and he let me know that he was a friend of Mother Theresa. I said to myself, "That's about as close as I will ever get to Sainthood."

Metz's Thoughts

One of the best things about Wendell was the woman he married, that being Priscilla Nowlin Baker.

Priscilla

I was born in Lexington to parents James and Mary Nowlin. I was one of ten children, eight boys and two girls. Like so many of the African American babies born at that time, I and six of my siblings were delivered by a midwife.

Growing up with that many brothers and a sister, there was never a lack of someone to play with, and doing so provided for a very happy childhood. We played marbles, rode bicycles, skated, sledded when it snowed, and just had a wonderful time growing up together. There weren't any cars, so we walked everywhere we went.

As many African Americans have suggested, our neighborhoods were full of caring parents. I remember that the parents in my neighborhood were all very concerned with the safety and well-being of all the children. They watched out for each other's children and even went so far as to correct or report misbehavior of children other than their own. "We took care of each other." That is a phrase that is often heard when remembering those days and even now.

With that many children, my mom stayed at home, and believe me there was plenty of work to do. She packed all our lunches: remember that would be ten lunches, and for some reason all the others in the family always wanted my lunch. They seemed to think it was the best lunch. I don't really think it was, but I do know my mom packed a wonderful lunch, and she was also a wonderful cook. She was also an excellent seamstress, so she did do some sewing for others.

We ironed all our clothes. My mother thought that was important, and with so many to iron for, that was an amazing feat. I learned how to iron because my mother insisted, and I still iron to this day. My children and others tease me because I still iron. They mostly just throw their clothes in the washer and take it out of the dryer and put it on going out the door. Sometimes they examine me for wrinkles just so they can give me a hard time about ironing.

I think I was fairly well liked by my classmates. I was in the band, many clubs, and I was a cheerleader. I also graduated from Lylburn Downing School, which is still very much a part of me. I remember my beautiful blue dress for the prom. My home economics teacher helped me make it. I loved it.

The Lylburn Downing "all purpose room," used for any and everything, is now a Community Room and is still used for many events. We have Lylburn Downing reunions, and that room is still a part of that.

After graduation, I went to work in a restaurant, and there of course was Wendell. He had a best friend who was called "Skipper." He and Wendell were inseparable and everyone wondered which one of them I was being courted by. Of course it was Wendell, and we ended up getting married in 1959. We have been married sixty years, and I think you could say it worked out very well. We have three children, Sheila, Marlene, and Wendell Baker III. The girls attended VCU and Wendell Jr. attended Hampton Institute. Education is very important to our family; we all went to college. Of this I am very proud!

We have always attended church, and we belong to First Baptist. That place has been a very important part of our family life, so we still support it. We also hold a reverence for the little old church Cedar Hill where many of our older members started out attending. There is a Cedar Hill reunion every year, and people come from all over to renew memories and family

Priscilla Nowlin Baker

and friendship ties. It is always out of doors with fried chicken, hamburgers, and every kind of potato salad and baked beans imaginable. Everyone brings something, and we pray, sing a little, and sit outside that tiny church just being thankful to be together.

The church has no electricity, so any service we have has to be in the daytime. It has a very old piano and memory books in the pulpit. The pews are hard and uncomfortable, but we don't mind. That's the way it was back when that church was filled with worshipers. There is also a cemetery some distance away from the church proper.

As our children were growing up, I decided to go back to school. It was not easy because I still had all the responsibilities of the home and raising three busy children. At first, I went through training at Stonewall Jackson Hospital to become a Licensed Practical Nurse, LPN. I finished that and worked in extended care. Then I decided to go back to school again to become a Registered Nurse. For that RN, I attended Blue Ridge College. For the next thirty-five years, I worked in medical surgical at the hospital. I also worked with geriatric patients at the close of my nursing career. I worked for Dr. McClung, Dr. Feddeman, Dr. Brush, Dr. Pleasants, and many others too numerous to list.

One outstanding memory that I must speak of is the election of Barack Obama to the presidency of the United States of America. I really never thought it would happen, at least not in my lifetime. I am glad I lived long enough for that and wish that some of our older family could have known of it.

Wendell & Priscilla Together

We have been so happy here in our life together. There are always those times that are rough. We think of the time when two of Priscilla's brothers were killed in an automobile accident. One had just returned from Afghanistan only to die here in Rockbridge County in a car. Those are the times when we most need each other.

We have lived right here in this house all these years. It was pasture land, no buildings, just cows. When we came to this house, the neighborhood was beginning to grow, and it was all black families. Now it is integrated. We have two white VMI families close to us.

We love our home and have made it comfortable for friends and family to visit. They will all come for Thanksgiving and Christmas. We always have a live tree that we put up in the corner of the living room next to the mantel. Our daughter comes over to decorate it, and we always say it is the prettiest one ever. We have wonderful grandchildren who never leave us without saying, "I love you." I am so grateful that they are the kind of people that are willing to say that out loud to their grandparents. We are very blessed and thankful for what we have and who we are.

Wendel's favorite foods are spaghetti and pot roast. I suppose I should stop and go cook one of those for supper.

Bless everyone!

"March on. Do not tarry. To go forward is to move
 toward perfection."

—*Khalil Gibran*

"Your daily life is your temple. When you enter it, take with you, your all."

—*Khalil Gibran*

Chapter 5
Lucy Evans Ferrebee

Metz's Note
When you enter the neat white Buena Vista home of Lucy Evans Ferrebee, you are struck by its character and warmth. It matches the essence of Lucy and what one might expect from a visit with her… it's inviting and interesting.

Lucy
I was born at home November 14, 1935, in Buena Vista, Virginia, to parents, Louis Blakey Evans and Preston Evans. My mother was from Buena Vista and my father from Collierstown, Virginia. I had a brother sixteen years younger, and because he came along so much later, I felt I was raised as an only child.

My mom's grandfather settled here in 1890 as a part of the boom. I knew my grandmother on my mother's side, but I was named for my father's mother, also Lucy.

We lived in the lower end of Buena Vista over the hill and into the mountain. It was wooded and beautiful, and we had so much fun going over the hills to pick berries. We would go

Lucy Evans Ferrebee

past the Old Buena Vista Colored School where my mother had gone to school as did my grandmother. That school is still very important to me, and I have worked with a dear friend, Irma Thompson, who taught there and has been instrumental in trying to restore it back to life as a museum. In fact, I am, at present, the secretary of the Colored School Board. We would so love to have it completed to honor Irma, who is 102 and has dedicated much of her life to that place.

I should tell you that I like to talk about things because I want to remember. I walked three miles to school, and it used to snow hard and often when I was growing up. Just thinking about walking to school in that snow makes my toes tingle.

I was a daydreamer. I loved to read, and being an only child, I shared many hours of reading with my father. I was an avid reader and was even in a book club, the only black child. We got books at the library too. My cousin Marylin Alexander's grandmother introduced her to the book club. I would buy books, and she would buy books. We would read them and then trade.

Books have always been my lifeline, and I like all kinds of books. I like mysteries, and I also like reading history and the Bible. I started my reading early, and that may be why I was wearing glasses by the time I was six years old.

History is so important, but many people don't seem to want to hear about it. We can't seem to get people out here interested in history. People, black people, do not seem to want to talk about the past. They just ignore it. Young blacks especially do not want to talk about the past.

My mother put her reading to a most important use when she read to a blind lady who lived out here. That lady was a friend of Helen Keller.

At that time, we had to use oil lamps for light, and one evening when we were reading, an oil lamp tipped over and caught my right eye. I have had much trouble with it ever since, and even now I find it limits my driving, my travel, and my sight.

My father was working hard in those years. He would drive over to the shipyard on the coast, and he also worked at the Delta Tau Delta fraternity house at Washington and Lee. My mother worked cleaning houses. From time to time, my father would say, "We've got to get out of here."

When I went into the seventh grade, I went in to Lexington to Lylburn Downing School. We had to get up very early, stand out in the cold because we were bussed in to school. After high school, I wanted to go to college. I was accepted to attend Hampton University, but things didn't work out for me to go, so I was looking for a job. I worked for a while in a restaurant near the post office in Lexington.

Then a very important thing happened that turned out to be one of the opportunities of my life. A close relative took me with her to New York. I had no real work experience and no particular training, so the possibility of finding employment was slim to none. But my relative had a job, a very good job, working for the Duchess of Denmark who was married to the Ambassador to Denmark. They had a summer home in upstate New York, and we all went there for the summer. I learned to cook. Another person in the house, Dorothy Hartwell, worked for them and a friend who was Secretary of State. We were meeting some very important people at that time.

First, there was a summer visit back home and then a return to New York. That short visit back home to Virginia and the mountains was followed by taking a job with Harry Lipsig. I took care of his mother-in-law. They lived in Hartsdale, New York.

One weekend, we went to a credit union convention in Buffalo, New York. I was aware of a job in North Tarrytown as a teller for General Motors Credit Union. I went for an interview. I got the job. I was thrilled.

After a fairly short time, the manager asked me if I thought I could manage the job. He explained that there were so many nationalities and so many different people, that he felt they were going to make it very hard for me.

I said, "I grew up in a neighborhood where I was the only black kid, and I managed just fine. I think I can manage this."

He gave me that opportunity to manage, and I did it! The NAACP said they had to have an African American, but I think they were really glad to have me. I was invited to all their parties, Italian, Jewish, you name it. I felt very accepted. I don't look at color—I look at who a person is inside, and that is what matters.

Well, I worked as a teller there for ten years. In the meantime, our office manager moved over to Bulova. I could have gone with him as he wanted me to go, but I stayed in Tarrytown. Our building was magnificent with a heliport on the roof. This was Rockefeller country and beautiful. My trips home every day went by the Old North Church. There were flowers everywhere.

Five years slipped by, and the next manager there suggested that I become the chief executive officer. I accepted. I posted 2,800 accounts on an old NCR accounting machine. Then we got computers, and I had a huge disc drive that I would take home with me for safety. There were those who did not want anything to do with the computers, but in time they of course became the way to do business.

We were required to continue our education and were provided the opportunity to utilize further study. In those years of intense brain work, I went to some notable places to keep up-to-date. In the decade of the seventies, I attended Elizabeth Seton in Yonkers, New York, and Iona University in New Rochelle, New York. I also attended some excellent programs at Cornell University. All of these programs focused on business in credit unions. Since I still had a full-time job, I attended classes on the weekends.

North Tarrytown was a small place with a Rockefeller presence. Duracell was there but then left. General Motors considered leaving but stayed a while longer. By then, I was referred to as "The Money Lady." That was partly because I had been there so long but also because I was very committed to the work I was doing. I would take work home, go early, stay late, and work as long and hard as it took to get it done.

At a certain point, I was given the task of finding a merger partner. I spent four years working on finding a partner for that merger. After considering AT&T, Pepsico, IBM, and Eileen Fisher, I finally chose Texaco.

Not only was I called "The Money Lady," I was still Miss Evans. I had never married. I had a very good friend whose wife had left him and he kept the children. Joseph Ferrebee and I were very supportive of each other, and we talked a lot. In fact, we talked during the next nineteen years.

Then the other shoe dropped. The GM Credit Union moved to Texas, and I had to make a hard decision as I did not want to make that particular move. I was devastated, partly because this was my family, my life. To make it worse, in the closure of our office, I lost everything, pension, vacation time ($30,000), sick leave, and other benefits. All were gone. The union could not help. I did not know what I should do. Stay in New York? Go back home to Virginia?

I finally thought I had made a decision, and I told Joe that I was going home to Virginia.

Joe said, "You can't go. Everyone loves you, and this is where you live."

I said, "No, I have to go back to the mountains."

He said, "Lucy, we've got mountains here." Then he said, "Lucy, I want you to marry me."

I said, "I'll think about it."

My mother said, "Lucy, say no, he's got kids."

But they were all gone. So I went to bed that night, and I thought hard. You can believe it or not but God said, "Lucy, say yes." And I did.

We got married in March and started to make a life of our own. He had a home, which we gutted and renovated and moved into in November. We had five years together until he was stricken with cancer. I said, "God, I don't know what you think, but you did tell me to say yes." Things have a way of working out, and fortunately I was the beneficiary of Joe's pension, the house, and social security.

By this time, I was sure it was time to go back home to Virginia. So I sold my house, packed up, and moved back home to the mountains in Buena Vista, Virginia. "BV," as they call it, is a beautiful spot, close to the mountains, home of a very nice liberal arts college, and best of all, my daughter. So I bought a house that I liked and have settled in for the long haul.

It didn't take long for me to get bored. Doing very little to nothing was not my style, and I soon decided to look for a job. There was a credit union "downtown" and so I applied for a position. They were not in the least impressed with all my years in New York as CEO of the GM Credit Union, or that I spent many summers at Cornell University in order to keep up with what was going on in the world of finance. They did not hire me.

So, I started a very active volunteer schedule. I volunteered at the Buena Vista Senior Center where I taught typing. I drive for Meals on Wheels and was elected to the board of VDFA (Virginia Department for Aging). I addressed health issues such as problems in my left eye, which now boasts the insertion of a titanium chip. I garden and take pride in the green additions of plant life that I have added to this home. I am now treasurer of AARP, and I am so proud to say that I was voted "Volunteer of the Year."

Many of my friends from New York stop off to see me on their way somewhere else. These are people like me who have retired from the various credit unions across the nation. Most of them were CEOs of those organizations and had major responsibilities to the members and those companies. I am also proud to be a part of this circle of professionals who also took their jobs very seriously.

One day I was working in the Senior Center here in BV, and a woman walked in the door. She looked at me carefully and finally said, "Who are you?"

Well, that was not what I had expected but I told her, and she said, "I know you."

I said, "I don't think so."

She continued to insist and finally after exchanging various forms of information, she said, "Honey, we're kin!" Sure enough we are related and that is an illustration of how often I run into people that are relatives or old friends from the past.

So it is that life has been good to me. I am comfortable with where I have been and what I have done. I continue to offer whatever ability I have to better the space I am in, and it has given me great joy. I embrace my daughter and my granddaughter and Irma Thompson and many other dear friends who have made life good. Memories are there for the pleasure that most of them provide. Friends do indeed make life worth living.

> "So long as memory of certain beloved friends lives in my heart, I shall say that life is good."
> —*Helen Keller*

Chapter 6

Margaret Joyce Henderson Wright

Metz's Note

I have known many wonderful people, but Margaret is truly a "woman of faith" who has served as a model for all who know her.

Margaret

I was born in 1931 in Blacksburg, Virginia, which is located between Buena Vista and Cornwall. My parents were James Marion Henderson, born in Lexington, and Flora Virginia Powell, born in Amherst, Virginia. I was the oldest of eight children, three sisters and four brothers. The boys were James Edward, Melvin Clinton, Elmer Eugene, and the baby, Clarence Hayward. The girls were Mary Isabella, Easter Marie (called Dee Dee), Druscilla Mae (called Goo Goo), and myself.

A wonderful woman named Rosa Wilson was the midwife who assisted my mother in the delivery of all her babies. Two were born in Lexington in Mudtown, later renamed Centerville. My father was one of four brothers, Matthew, Floyd, Hugh, Henderson, and my father.

Margaret Joyce Henderson Wright

My grandfather was married twice, first to a lady named Margaret Coleman related to the Alex Woods who lived on Tucker Street. Later, he was married to my grandmother who was American Indian of the Blackfoot Tribe. She had the most amazing hair. It was so long that she could sit on it. My mother's brother was Jasper Powell.

Our childhood was rough, very rough. We lived out in the country and made our living off the land. The land was owned by a white farmer, and he was actually very good to us, letting us live there, farm, eat the products. But we had no lights, only an oil lamp, and we had to cut down trees for firewood to make fires for warmth. I had to iron, and it was not easy or safe. You had to put the iron on the stove and let it get hot and then move it over to the piece that you were going to iron. We had a well, which meant that the water had to be hauled. My mother had chickens, which did provide eggs and later a chicken dinner.

There was a terrible incident that happened to me, and at the time I didn't understand it. My brother and I went out to walk in the woods, and we were supposed to get home before dark. I had the most uneasy feeling, very afraid, and I said to my brother, "Brother, there is someone behind us." I thought I could see the outline of a man behind us, and I said, "Let's let him pass." But then he disappeared into the deeper woods.

Years later, it became clear to me that this was not danger coming to us. It was an angel that I was to fully understand long afterward. I was to learn that I had a destiny to fulfill, but at the time, I thought it was one of the gypsies that lived in the area. They were strange and would pick up children. We were all afraid of them.

We, of course, had to walk everywhere we went and usually through the woods. There in Cornwall we had to climb over a fence, and one day my mother and I were chased by a white man. I ran and got well ahead of her, but I heard her call out, "Wait for me." I waited for her, and she caught up, and we escaped that situation. I cannot account for the fact that this is so much a part of my memories but it is.

I was the strongest, and I suppose because I was the oldest, I had more responsibilities. I had most of the chores. At times I thought, "Let my brother do it." But even with all the work given me, I did not take it personally. I knew I had better do what I was supposed to do.

Much later in my life, my grandson asked me this question:. "What about the white people? How did they treat you?"

I said, "They were good to us." We never feared them. And I must say that is a feeling I strongly hold today. I am not afraid and bear no ill will.

When asked how it was to grow up during segregation, I answer, "Just fine." We did not see or feel the negativity. I must say that progress was made for a time, but now in the present we have gone backwards. We have lost that progress, and it is reinforced in the political life of this nation.

We went to school in the country. It was a one room school with five grades. Our teacher, Ms. Dorothy McCutcheon, taught all five grades, and that must have been very difficult for her. She would teach a grade while the others completed assignments, and then she would move to the next grade level. She was a good teacher.

In 1943, we moved to Lexington, and I entered Lylburn Downing School. I did not finish, and I have always regretted that. I would have liked to go on, but World War II came along and I decided I wanted to be a WAC—that was the Women's Army Corps. I wanted to be a soldier to serve my country. But due to the lack of education, I was not accepted and had to consider other options.

I had many jobs during those years starting at $1.25 an hour. I worked as a waitress. There was the Officer's Candidate School at Washington and Lee, and Alex Wood was there. Many of the jobs I had were hard labor. For sixteen years, I worked for one family, the Bargers. And then I worked at one of the fraternity houses for many years, and at the Robert E. Lee Hotel. Leslie Cauthern got me that job. Tiny Hughes was the cook. I worked in the dining room, and I loved that, doing something tangible. I also worked at the Lexington Country Club. Doug Gardner got me that job. I would walk from 21 Fuller Street out to the Golf and Country Club. That was a long walk to and from the job.

Another job was at the Heritage Nursing Home. Mrs. Inez Coffey interviewed me as I was sitting on a milk carton.

At one point I asked, "If I am hired, when would I start?"

She said, "You are hired, and you start now!"

I was thrilled because I was making $7.25 an hour.

I met my first husband, Joseph Ronald Harris, and together we had a daughter, Joanna. But my life with him was both frightening and confusing. At one point in our relationship, he abducted me and took me to Chicago. There were times that I should have been very frightened, but I was not. I was depending on God to protect me. My husband ended up giving me the money to get a ticket home. He was a very unstable person who was into very serious trouble, which ultimately led to his suicide.

Years later, I met James Wright. We had our own children, five to be exact. They are Jacqueline, Isadora, Valentina (Val), Andrea Marie, and one boy, Paul Ellis Henderson. But there were serious problems in that marriage too, and ultimately we separated. I considered a divorce but decided against it. We remain separated after many years. I determined that this was what God had ordained for me.

The children and I lived with my mother for a time. She was a maid at the Robert E. Lee Hotel. It was crowded, and we still had only the basic needs. We still had a wood stove. I knew that we needed to get out and find a place of our own and strive for a better life. We did move, and we first lived at 21 Fuller Street. Later, we moved to 218 Fuller Street, obtaining that property from Ms. Nelly White.

All my children have done well and made me exceedingly proud. They are smart, they are educated, and they are thoughtful. I know more in my old age than I did earlier. I was, however, able to instill certain values that I hope have served them well throughout their lives. I have tried to model a life of faith and belief that will serve them in all situations. I have told my children that "not all white people are bad and not all black people are your friend." Today is in alignment with the prophecy of the Bible. I believe we have to go back to God.

Technology today is being abused. It is a good thing, but never in my life did I think I would see such things as everyone walking around tied to a phone. They have forgotten how to imagine or how to interact socially.

My thoughts today carry me back in time to the day when I thought someone was following me. Now I realize that someone was following me and inviting me to follow them. It was Jesus Christ in God through an angel inviting me to follow my destiny.

Now that the children are living their own lives, I have turned more and more to serving the church. It is my life! I proudly serve both as treasurer of my church and also as a Mother of the Church, which is a great honor.

My church building is old and historically significant. It is among one of the oldest structures in Lexington. Originally known as Saint Patrick's Catholic Church and Diocese, it was and still is located at 109 Henry Street, Lexington, Virginia. Let me share some of its story, which I found in a publication about the church.

Before a parish was formally established in Lexington, Catholics had attended mass either in private homes or in the Lexington Fire Engine House at the corner of Randolph and Washington Streets. One of those homes was the Edward Hefrin residence at 207 Randolph Street.

In 1873, a parish was formed largely through the efforts of a man named John Sheridan. Construction of this structure began that same year on a plot 50 feet along Henry and 100 feet deep, purchased from Mr. and Mrs. Joseph Fuller for $285. The cost of the structure, furnished with pews for seating seventy-five, was $2,934. The number of parishioners who were listed in 1874 was eighty-three.

That number waxed and waned, and by 1898, there were only twenty-six members. From 1893 until 1946, the parish was without a priest. Years passed and in 1952, ground was broken for the new location of Saint Patrick's Church.

To help reduce the debt for the new structure, it was decided to sell the original church building. It sold for $15,000 to the

Lexington Telephone company. Today, in 2019, the property is owned by yet another church, known as Gospel Way Church of God in Christ.

This is my church. This is my life. I have devoted much of my energy and spirit to the stabilization and improvement of this church. This is an active congregation with a vibrant pastor, a choir, a youth choir, and a technical staff, but above all a dedication to the power of the Holy Spirit, Christ Jesus, and living the Christian life.

My belief is to walk in our destiny. I look forward to the "generation of blessing," regardless of what they have done, there is a blessing in everyone.

> "People leave traces of themselves where they feel most comfortable, most worthwhile."
> —*Hauki Murakami*

Chapter 7
Maria Elizabeth McLellan Quillin

Metz's Note
Funny, lively, intelligent, gutsy… a firecracker with a great big heart and an intelligence to lead the way. No one can really describe Maria. She defies description. Oh, and yes, she is beautiful inside and out!

Maria
I was born on January 22, 1940, at the old Stonewall Jackson Hospital in Lexington, Virginia. My father was William Douglas McLellan, originally from Pittsburgh, Pennsylvania, and my mother, Reada Lucille Blak, came from the Eastern Shore in Maryland.

Early in my life, we moved to Pittsburgh because my father had a job in the steel mill. We lived in the projects in what reminded me of barracks set up in rows. We were lucky because we were on the end so we had windows all around. It seemed like the sky was orange all the time.

There was lots of grass and lots of kids. My sister, Margaret Cecelia McClellan, was my little buddy. I called her "Bootie." In fact I took care of her. I was then and am now her "protector." Nobody messed with my baby sister because they would have to deal with me if they did. She used to suck her two middle fingers and have mud running down her chin.

We walked to school, and winters in Pittsburgh were really cold. My mom made me wear a hat that I hated. I called it my Sherlock Holmes hat, and my mom practically tied me in it. It had flaps in the front and in the back, and it looked like that red hat Elmer Fudd used to wear in the cartoons. I am sure I looked like a cartoon. I would struggle to take it off and then make sure it was back on my head before I went home to my mother. I also had some black and white saddle oxfords, which I liked somewhat better.

We loved to play outside. I was pretty daring. In fact, I was a tomboy. I had a three-wheel bicycle that had a chain. I would fly up and down a nearby hill with my sister on the back. I was a demon flying down the hill. One time the chain broke, and I had to fix it. I wasn't sure how to do it, but I figured it out.

I am trying to remember some things about the school I attended. I guess it was all black, not integrated, but I really can't remember. I guess that's good because it left no impression on me, certainly not anything unpleasant. I do remember having lunch, sitting on the floor in the classroom.

We would visit my uncle, John Scott, at 108 E. Preston in Lexington in the summers. I loved that house and all its familiar touches. I could actually smell my family! My uncle had many cats.

Maria Elizabeth McLellan Quillin

Eventually, we moved back to Lexington. It was really good to get back to friends and relatives. My dad was a cook or maintenance worker at Washington and Lee. I was enrolled in Lylburn Downing School, which was all black, still segregated. There was this one big room that had expandable walls.

I was good at getting into trouble. I guess you could say I made waves. Back in those days if we misbehaved, we got punished, and more than once I got my hand smacked with a ruler. I called it "corporal punishment." They could not do such these days; there would be lawsuits galore.

One time, I wore a very thick skirt with many layers underneath because it was cold. Of course, I did get into trouble that day and got called in for "corporal punishment." This time I got spanks on the back end, but because of all that thick clothing, I could barely feel it. However, I made great noise as if it hurt. I was also a pretty good actress. But the bad thing about those times was that after getting it at school, I also would get it when I got home.

Back then in our neighborhood, the adults were in charge, and they would not only take care of us, they would spread the word if we got in trouble. We all took care of each other and still do. The grownups knew if we misbehaved, and even if they were not our parents, they knew they were obliged to reprimand us. It was so different then.

While we were still at Lylburn Downing, integration took place, but they still were not set up to accommodate the new plan. We had to spend half the day at Lylburn Downing and then walked to the high school for the rest of the day. My sister and I did just fine with this as we were used to being self-reliant.

Sandwiched in the Lylburn Downing days was our military adventure. My biological father was a "rolling stone." Eventually my mother and dad divorced and later mother married Harold Jackson. He was in the military, and we got transferred to Fort Huachuca, Arizona. He had a tendency to get into trouble too, so his rank did not provide transportation for his dependents, and he would go on ahead of us.

My mom, sister, and I would take the Greyhound bus out to Arizona. It must have been a long trip taking several days. We loved the trip but would get restless. On rest stops, we would have to do something to stretch our legs. We had a pair of skates. I wore one skate and my sister wore the other. It was crazy but fun. My mom was in charge of everything and she took good care.

Being a military family, we moved so much. Next we went to Fort Lewis in Washington State. We went to Germany more than once. All these moves were hard on our education, but we did graduate from Lylburn Downing. I should have gone to college at that time, but instead my mom and I worked at a sorority house at Washington and Lee.

In July of 1969, I had a baby girl. She was critically ill throughout her life. When she was two years old, she was at the University of Virginia Medical School Hospital where she was diagnosed with Von Recklinhauser disease, a genetic disorder characterized by tumors on nerves. It can also affect the skin and deform bones. She was very sick. I married her father, Charles Wilson Pennick, to give her a name and shortly after, had the marriage annulled. Then her name was Kelly Ann Pennick.

Kelly Ann and I moved in with my mom. When Kelly was five years old, I married Guy D. Hunt and had two more children, Douglas Guy Hunt and Michael Hunt. Since Guy was in the military, we all shipped out to Germany. Kelly Ann did well enough to join the Girl Scouts, and she enjoyed it while she could.

Later back in Virginia, the doctors at University of Virginia Medical School wanted to do surgery on Kelly Ann. It was determined that it would be done at Walter Reed Hospital in Washington, DC. We were flown there on MATS (Military Air Transportation Service.) Those were difficult days. I still have a little coloring book that I bought her to help pass the time. But her condition worsened, and she died at Walter Reed. We brought her back to Lexington for her final resting place. Meanwhile, her Scout group back in Germany placed a special brick in her honor at the Girl Scout Headquarters. She lived eleven years and six months.

By 1973, I was back in Lexington working for Dr. Len Jarrard as a lab assistant. The focus was research on memory and learning. I trained the rats used in the experiments. That was difficult because I hated having to euthanize the rats. I recall being there in that laboratory at Washington and Lee at the same time that Ted DeLaney was there taking courses. Because it was an all-male school, I was not eligible for the same credit that would have been given a male. Feeling that inequity of reward, I joined the army!

Things were not going so well by then, and I divorced Guy Hunt. This was another disappointment, but as often happens, it turned out well in the long run. My years in the army provided opportunities that I would not have had otherwise, and one of those was still present in the form of my service after I was given an honorable discharge. However, I continued my annual two-week reserve commitment, and my experience and education were further enhanced.

One opportunity was that of becoming a teaching assistant in the Rockbridge school system. I was encouraged to get my degree, which I did through Mary Baldwin College. I then got a masters at Virginia Tech, so I am officially a "Hokie."

Then an amazing thing happened. One day, I went to the library there in Lexington. Little did I expect that there on that day I would meet "my soul mate." My future mate was a man named T. Ajene Quillin, (pronounced Ah-jen-aay, French). He had a gold tooth that twinkled at me, and when I learned that he rode a motorcycle…that did it! He was "It."

I had also taken up motorcycling, and to have this unexpected riding companion was just too wonderful. Ajene had come to Lexington with a group of "numerologists." He lived in a shack by the boat locks near Buena Vista. Although I was clearly smitten, I hesitated to make a permanent commitment for the next six years. I had been down the marital road and was shy about doing that again.

Along with his shining gold tooth and an abundance of charm, I learned that he was also educated and an activist. He had a degree in sociology and had worked in community awareness programs in Chicago. He wrote and had articles published on social problems. He was in a writing group in Lexington.

We were together for thirty years, twenty-two years married. He retired in 2006, and we had great plans to travel. But that was sadly not to be when he was diagnosed with Parkinson's disease. That progressed and was further complicated with Alzheimer's. I became the caregiver for as long as it was possible. He was in several nursing homes, the last being Crossroads in Petersburg (suggested for combative patients). There he had a stroke and died of pneumonia.

He was my soul mate, my true love, and I am grateful for the years we had together. It was a "long goodbye."

Now I am a widow, and I take care of my sister who was also brought down with Alzheimer's. She is hardly recognizable from the vibrant young woman who spent years as an air traffic controller for the Federal Aviation Administration, who stood up for black women in the industry without breaking the union picket line, and had a full experience with the "glass ceiling." She is with me for the long haul, and she is still my baby sister—I am still her protector.

I stay active in the church. I have so many interests, one of which involves building a studio in my backyard for my own pleasure and that of others. I have had a life I am happy with and made some mistakes as we humans are prone to do, but all in all, I feel blessed with people, talent, curiosity, energy, and I say—that is enough for me.

"Always try to keep a patch of the sky above your life."
—*Marcel Proust*

Chapter 8

Irene Elizabeth Pennick Thompson

Metz's Note

My friend Irene always referred to herself as a caregiver. That she truly is. She has spent her life taking care of others. She has come to see it as a preordained blessing, a gift, an inspiration. And she has lived up to it her whole life.

Irene

I was born April 1, 1940, in a house at 4 Perry Lane, which has since been renamed Parry Lane. My mother, Elaine Hall Pennick, was assisted in that delivery by a midwife. While my mother was from Lexington, my father, Charles Wilson Pennick, was originally from Dayton, Ohio. My father worked in a steel mill in Ohio but came to Lexington to attend a funeral. He stayed long enough to marry my mother. From this marriage, two children were born, my brother, Charles Erskine Pennick, and twenty months later, I was born.

My father was a "rolling stone." He loved boxing and was very good at it, so I hear. I could not be sure because I only remember seeing him a few times in my life. Once when I was four years old and after I was graduated from high school and then I went to Dayton, Ohio, in search of him.

My brother Charles and I loved to play outdoors and had fun playing hide-and-seek and poking sticks at the turtles in the creek that ran past our house. In the winter, we loved to get on a sled and slide down one of the many hills.

For the most part, life was pretty good. My mother worked part time, but on Sunday we would take walks along the Maury River, go for rides on the Blue Ridge Parkway, attend church, and go on country outings. I especially remember the delicious Sunday dinners.

I was a member of a club called "Willing Workers," and we had many activities. We would go to Goshen Pass, and most others would swim, but because I did not ever learn to swim, I just waded but loved it.

Once, when I was just a little girl, my brother Charles and I were visiting in the garden of a woman who had a lovely little granddaughter, Suzanne Barksdale (Rice), who was about three years old. I remember sitting on the steps of the porch with the two of them. Very recently I encountered Suzanne as an adult, and we were astounded to reconnect remembering vividly that wonderful day. Someone took our picture, and she still has hers, which she has kept all those years.

When I was twelve years old, my grandmother was called upon to go to Cincinnati, Ohio, to take care of an ailing sister-in-law. Those years were the best of my life, my happiest memories as a child. We stayed in this big three-story house in Walnut Hills. It was here that I learned the joy of music, art, and literature. I attended school there, and I enjoyed it. That joy is still with me

Irene Elizabeth Pennick Thompson

today, and I owe it all to the exposure I had during that time in Cincinnati.

Shortly after I arrived in Cincinnati, the Isley Brothers music group was formed, and my best friend had a crush on Ronald Isley. My friend and I had many great adventures and experiences such as walking up Victory Parkway to downtown Cincinnati, going to Walnut Hills library, walking to Eden Park overlooking the Ohio River, and especially visiting the Cincinnati Conservatory of Music guest performances.

Augustus Dawson was that friend that shared all these experiences. We enjoyed the boats going up and down the Ohio River, we enjoyed talks about everything but especially the peaceful surroundings.

Years later when I had to leave Cincinnati, we walked to Eden Park to say our goodbyes and to make a vow that we would never lose touch with each other. We kept that vow.

I returned there for her wedding; she then returned to Lexington for her honeymoon, which was spent at the Jordan Tourist Home on Main Street. I lived two doors down from the Tourist Home.

Through the years, we visited each other and realized that our four children were the same ages. That was incredible. Each time I would visit Cincinnati, we would return to Eden Park.

Five years ago, when she was dying from ALS, I went to visit her and to hold her hand and relive some of our precious memories. Through tears, I told her that the next time we would be together, it would not be in Eden Park but it would be in the Garden of Eden.

I had another friend, Lucy Jordan from Fayetteville, North Carolina. I mention her because she used to say to me, "You enjoyed the arts and music so much in Cincinnati; you should get out and go places more often."

Leaving Cincinnati had been hard, but the time came for us to go back to Lexington. I was enrolled in Lylburn Downing School. I thought it was fine. We had good teachers who really seemed to care about us as people, not just kids who would come and go. I still remember my senior prom. In fact, I attended two or three senior proms—my own during my senior year and the proms of others who were nice enough to invite me.

I remember my beautiful prom dress. The dress was pink satin with a flaring skirt worn over crinolines. I had a beautiful carnation corsage, and Samantha Poindexter did my hair in a beautiful wave page-boy style.

The prom itself was simply magnificent! The theme that year was "Sweethearts on Parade." It was truly splendid, decorated with hearts and streamers and providing a great atmosphere. It was held in what is now called the Community Room at Lylburn Downing.

The most exciting part of the prom was that I danced with Lewis Watts! Wow! Lewis was and is a true hero of our town of Lexington. He was an amazing young man. He had no arms! He was a member of a band, the lead singer, in a group called The Rhythm Makers. (My husband to be was also in that group, but I will tell you about that later.) Lewis did not let anything hold him back. He could play baseball and write with his feet in a beautiful penmanship. He was a man of courage, talent, and integrity.

It was at another dance, a sock hop, that I danced again, but this time it was with the man who many years later would become my husband, Vaden Hamilton Thompson Jr. A mutual friend of each of us made the introduction, and we hit it off there on the dance floor. We started to spend time together. We mostly went to activities and worship services at our respective churches. I was and still am Baptist, and he is Methodist. So we went to BTU (Baptist Training Union) at my church on Main Street and to MYF (Methodist Youth Fellowship) at his church on Randolph Street.

He became very devoted to the previously mentioned band called The Rhythm Makers. He played the drums and the keyboard and is still well remembered for his role in that group. He was given a nickname, Sticks. Of course that was because he played the drums.

We dated from 1957 until 1964 when we got married in Augusta, Georgia. I wore a suit as it was Easter, and Margaret Scott, here in Lexington, made it for me. It was an ivory suit with a bolero jacket. I called it my "Easter suit."

It was about that time that I started writing my chronicles, and I have kept up with them throughout my life. These are simply records of my life and the things that happened along the way. I have always called myself a caregiver. Thankfully, somewhere along the way I realized I was ordained to give care to others. That was my calling, and I thank God for that.

So it was that we were living in Lexington, and my husband was working for Greyhound Bus Lines. In 1966, we had our first son, Randall Lee Thompson. In 1968, Vaden Hamilton Thompson III was born. Our third son came along and his name, which he chose himself later in life as a Muslim, is Wahid Warsaw Shabazd. He and his wife have six children. My next son has five children and the youngest has two.

Nine years after the third son came along, our daughter was born. Rachelle Lynn Thompson Ferrer and I are very close. After she graduated from James Madison University, she became a project manager for Coca-Cola Company. I love being with her. I am equally proud of my sons. They are all wonderful, loving, and devoted men. Randall Lee has five children, and Vaden the third has two.

I am now taking care of my brother who is in a nursing facility in Salem, Virginia. I go there regularly to take things he needs, visit, and provide him with a care box that I fill with various things, hopefully to brighten his day. He loves fried chicken and potato salad, so I try to take these and other favorites.

I am not sure how many more people there will be for me to give care to, but I will be there as long as possible if needed. I will continue my devotion and commitment to the church, fulfill the duties of deacon, which I have accepted. I am currently working on a big project programing the church archives. I will love God and be grateful for the ability with which I was blessed to give care wherever it is needed.

> "Someday many years from now, we'll sit beside the candle's glow exchanging tales about our past and laughing as the memories flow. And when that distant day arrives, I know it will be understood that friendship is the key to life and we were friends and it was good."
>
> —*Eileen Hehl*

Chapter 9
Vaden Hamilton Thompson Jr.

Metz's Note

Vaden Hamilton Thompson Jr. is the descendant of slaves who worked at Buffalo Forge. He is also the husband of Irene Thompson from the previous chapter. An articulate man who understands what life is all about, he sure could play the drums. I am proud to have known this talented individual.

Vaden

I was born March 29, 1941, in Lexington. My father was Vaden Thompson Sr., of Lexington, and my mother was Cornelia Massie, whose father was named General Lee Massie. I grew up in Lexington, the oldest of seven children, the other six being girls: Elizabeth Lee, Angeline, Sandra Kay, Linda, Gwendolyn, and Rose Marie. I could tell you many stories about being the only boy with six younger sisters. Ours was a big family, and we enjoyed being together.

A big part of our family story began with my great-grandfather, Garland Thompson, whose story is told in great detail in Chapter 6 of Charles B. Dew's book, *Bond of Iron*. It describes the Thompsons as typical of many slave iron-working families at Buffalo Forge. In reading the book, we learned that William Weaver purchased Garland Thompson, my great-grandfather, who was a strong slave forgeman, who was then married to one of Weaver's slave women.

According to *Bond of Iron*, the story of this slave family is typical, and it is made all the more fascinating to me that an oral history among Garland Thompson's descendants in the Valley is my own.

Dew writes that Garland used his extra earnings to improve his family's standard of living. The first page of Garland's account in the surviving "Negro Books" describes him buying coffee, sugar, cotton cloth, and a pitcher. Then on December 24, 1830, he spent $13 on "Goods etc. for Christmas."

Christmas still has special meaning for our family. We celebrated all holidays together, remembering each other in special ways. Those holidays were a big deal. Because there were so many of us, we needed a large house. First, we lived at 112 Moore Street. Then we moved to a larger place at 114 Davidson Street. My mom had plenty to keep her busy, but as we grew up she started work as a housekeeper. After that she became a dispatcher for the Lexington Police Department. My father was a chef and cooked in many of the well-known restaurants in the area.

I attended Lylburn Downing School, and it was there that I found two great joys of life. The first was Miss Irene Pennick. I first knew her through her brother, Charles Pennick, but we danced at a sock hop, and I walked her home. I often tell the story about why I was most impressed with her. I said it was

Vaden Hamilton Thompson Jr.

because she didn't kiss me. Much later she said, "Now why on earth would I want to kiss you?"

We visited each other's churches. For her it was the Baptist Church with the BTU (Baptist Training Union) and for me it was MYF (Methodist Youth Fellowship) at the Randolph Street Methodist Church. We belonged to Willing Workers, a group that visited the sick, the elderly, and shut-ins. We went on hayrides and outings on the river and just had fun. After I graduated from Lylburn Downing, I had gone into the army. I was stationed at Fort Devins, Massachusetts. Irene and I got married March 29, 1964, in Augusta, Georgia. I went to work for Grayhound Bus Lines. Later, I went to work for the Abbot Bus Lines. I am "on call" to drive special charter assignments. I drive the VMI cadets as well as other college and university groups.

The other joy discovered was music, in the form of a band called The Rhythm Makers, which was just about the most exciting thing I have ever done. I graduated from high school in 1960, but I joined The Rhythm Makers in 1956.

The group was formed from the high school band and was started by the principal, Ulysses Broadneau Sr. After hearing us play, he said, "You boys sure can make rhythm." We liked what he said and decided that would be our name, The Rhythm Makers.

Our first gig was for a school dance, and they paid us $50. We played the college and university circuit mostly, and we were in demand. In 1980, we played in Carnegie Hall and then the Apollo Theater in Harlem, New York. We mostly played rhythm and blues, and we really liked to "jam."

Life on the road was hard, especially before the public accommodation laws were passed. We couldn't find a place that would let us come in and eat or sleep. We could always count on, and go into, the black communities, but they were usually on the back roads. There was no facility on the main roads that would serve the band. We had to sleep in the car, and it was very crowded. We had an old 1955 model Ford. We used the transmission to heat our food, mostly Vienna sausage and cans of beans.

The band was very popular and included Bill Hoffman on guitar, myself on the drums, Ulysses "Junior" Broadneaux on saxophone, Frank Woodley on keyboard, Napoleon "Teddy" Borgus on trombone, and Lewis Watts the vocalist. Lewis had no arms to play an instrument, but he could really belt out a song. The band was all black until Don East joined the group. Because I played the drums, I was given the nickname "Sticks," and I am still called that today.

We have a lovely family, three boys and a girl, but I know Irene has told you about that.

I am proud of my family, wife, children, parents, and sisters. Life is good.

As far as segregation was concerned, we were sensitive to it, but we didn't think much about the term racism. That's just the way it was. But at least, during segregation, we had our own identity. When the Lylburn Downing band marched down Main Street, everyone stopped and yelled and clapped because they liked seeing and hearing us. Our memories are with us forever.

"Life brings tears, smiles, and memories. The tears dry, the smile fades, but the memories last forever."
—*Malik Faisal*

Chapter 10

Leon Harvey

Metz's Note

This man faced many hardships throughout his life, but he found the one and only way that worked for him to survive. I so admire his desire to make the necessary changes that kept him going.

Leon

I was born on Christmas day, December 25, 1935, at 107 Diamond Street in Lexington. My father was James Harvey, and my mother was Lucy Virginia Ware. I had one brother, James Harvey, who was older and a sister, Cynthia, who was younger, and not a Harvey. My father committed suicide when I was a year and a half, and that single event was an ever-present undercurrent of my life. Even though I was so young when it happened, the lack of male guidance caused great anger and resentment on my part, and it showed in every part of my life.

We were dirt poor. We had nothing. I had three aunts who all had illegitimate children. My grandmother Ware ended up raising all those children and me. There were nine kids for her to raise. I was very difficult, hard to deal with, defiant, and disrespectful. Everyone was poor then, and I remember how painful it was for me to go to school. I hated school! I had no clothes. I would have to put cardboard in my shoes, drive a nail through the sole, push a wire, and bend it back to keep my shoes together.

I really dreaded school. I couldn't learn because I was filled with shame. At home, we didn't have facilities for personal hygiene, so I am sure I smelled bad. I was filled with anger, and I was constantly in trouble. Any male was a challenge to me, and I resisted any and all attempts to control me. To hide my shame, I became a wise guy who fought any and all discipline. I wanted to quit school, but back in those days, you were required to go until the age of sixteen, but the day I turned sixteen, I quit! I was a "smart-a—." I look back and hate the person I was for many years following. I was sixteen years old and in the sixth grade! I just could not learn. I was so filled with self-doubt. I had to go to work.

My first job was as a dishwasher at Virginia Beach. I washed so many dishes, all by hand. I finally went back to Lexington and got a job working in the VMI Post Exchange restaurant. I made sandwiches and cleaned the floor. Every dime I had was spent on alcohol and pot. I was still a wise guy and probably obnoxious to all around me.

When I was eighteen years old, I joined the army. I was first stationed at Fort Jackson, Columbia, South Carolina, with the 101st Airborne. Then I went to Camp Chaffee at Fort Smith, Arkansas, in the field artillery, then Fort Lewis in Washington State. Some people may have hated being in the army, but I loved it!

Leon Harvey

For the first time in my life, I had a bed I could sleep in by myself with clean sheets, take a shower, wear clothes that were new, shoes that didn't have to be wired together, and meals that were prepared. It was the best I had ever lived. The most significant thing was that the resistance to male authority finally subsided as I just did what I was told and it worked for me. I would have stayed in the army, but I didn't have enough education for them to want me, but at that time I was a good soldier.

Since staying in the service was not one of my choices, I went back to Lexington. I went to work at VMI. I met a girl named Annie Mae. I married her out in Glasgow in the preacher's home, and sometime later became the father of two daughters. One lives in Lexington and the other in Texas. I have grandchildren: four boys and three girls.

I have always attended the First Baptist Church in Lexington. One day, maybe in Sunday School, I heard that you couldn't go to heaven if you hadn't been baptized. So I ran down and got myself baptized. So even though I was baptized, I was probably still drinking and smoking all the time. I drank too much for sure. I was still pretty much a mess.

But December 19, 1982, was the day my life changed forever! I was watching television and the preacher on the program said, "If you drink and smoke you are violating the temple of God." Well, I thought he meant the temple was a building. The preacher said, "The temple of God is your body!" For some reason that I cannot explain, that made a huge difference, thinking I was violating the temple of God.

I went home and got down on my knees and prayed and prayed. I asked God to help me find a way to put aside the anguish and discontent that had been so much a part of my life. I recalled the time I too had considered suicide even though I hated the thought since my father had killed himself. At that time, I had decided to carry a gun at all times. Oddly enough, the very day I had planned to kill myself, I had left the gun in the car, which was unusual. As I sat on the side of that bed, I decided to go to the car and get that gun. But when I tried to get up, I couldn't move! I was paralyzed from the waist down. My wife called the preacher to come and pray. Through that prayer, God spoke to my spirit. I let go of the plan of suicide, and I could walk.

So I got up from my knees with a feeling of being cleansed and free. From that moment on, I went to the church in earnest and started to read the Bible. My life changed forever. I love the Bible, especially the Psalms.

Times were still hard. My wife and I were renting a house on Massie Street, and we prayed that the Lord would give us the means to have a house of our own, and He did. We bought our home here at 410 Maury for which we were grateful, and still I am grateful.

I went to work at W&L in Evans Hall. I got into cooking and from there went to work for the VMI Food Service. I had also done some cooking at the Country Club. When the Food Service lost their contract at VMI, I went to work at the Phi Delta Theta Fraternity House. There I met a young man from Mobile, Alabama. At the time, I did not realize what an impact he would have on my life. I have been blessed by many and this one young man stands out above all others.

When I consider all that he has meant to me, I wonder what I might have done to deserve such caring and love. He graduated and left, but when he would come back to W&L events, he would always come to see me, take me to lunch, and revisit old times together at the fraternity house.

Times were hard again. My wife was diagnosed with cancer, and we had no insurance. The medical bills were staggering, and I had maxed all our credit cards to the limit. I was deeply worried about how to manage this situation. I actually could see no way.

My young friend John, from the fraternity, must have sensed the darkness I was in, and after a visit to Lexington, he called and said, "Leon, I can see that you are in some financial trouble. With your social security, how much would you need to live and to clear up all your debts?" I told him and he said, "Help is on the way. Send me the bills you owe, medical, credit cards, anything that needs to be paid."

He then paid it all and started to send $400 a month from then on. He said, "I know you need a car, and I am calling the Chevrolet dealer to get you one." To this day, he sends a check at Thanksgiving and Christmas.

Looking back, I suppose I helped him in some ways when he was young and foolish, just as I had been with too much carousing, drinking, and smoking—too much of everything. There were times when I was there to keep him out of trouble, but I never would have imagined the kind of return I received.

John became ill himself at one point, and he called late one night and asked me to pray with him. God did not see that as John's time to go, and he was able to overcome the problems of his health. He is my friend in Christ, and we pray, sometimes over the phone. We are saved.

But all was not well. My wife had been diagnosed with cancer and died too soon. I was to be alone for a long time, except for my daughters.

There was yet another blessing that I must mention. There are five people in Richmond that I have been so fortunate to know. I met them at a summer camp where they were all counselors. One is now a doctor, another a lawyer, and three are educators in universities. They have maintained our friendship through the years and helped out when they saw a need. One bought us a freezer; another helped put a shower in our bathroom. They touched my life and still do.

White folks were good to me. I never had any trouble with white folks. We had a white family across the street, and they were the only ones that stand out. They would scream at their children and say, "I told you to stay away from those damn n—." The man would come home every Friday night, sit out on the porch, get drunk, and then go in and beat his wife. He beat her every week. She would then come over bloodied and hysterical and ask for help. My grandmother Ware would not allow us to be bothered by it. She always said, "You don't go anywhere you are not wanted."

Human caring and touching are vital to the growth of the spirit. I remember as a child when I had an attack of acute appendicitis. There was a white doctor here in Lexington, and he was known for his drinking. I was desperately in need of medical attention, and my grandmother hesitated but called this doctor. He was available, but she was worried that he might be drinking. He was sober! He took care of me! He hugged me! As a small child, I could feel his sincerity and compassion. He touched me with a reassurance that I needed and still remember.

Now, I recall how I believe in truth. I was messed up as a kid. The business of Christmas with Santa Claus is a lie. I was told that the good kids would get what they asked for. There were plenty of really bad kids in our neighborhood, and while we got nothing, those bad kids got bicycles and roller skates. That was a lie to me. There was no Santa Claus, and I would never tell my kids that there was. I resented the idea of a Christmas tree and decorations when the emphasis should be on the birth of Jesus. This is what I told my own children, and I am not sure how that played out in their own thoughts, but I had to do what I believed.

Now I have diabetes, I can't see to read, and am almost blind. Most of my friends have died or are gone. I have no education, but the Lord has given me an understanding and let me get this far. For me the truth is in God. I hope you have a blessed day.

> "The Lord is my Shepherd
> I shall not want,
> He makes me lie down
> In green pastures,
> He restores my soul."
> —*From the 23rd Psalm*

Chapter 11

Tuney & Tick

It was late and the sun was bidding its farewell until another day. Tuney and Tick were seated at the kitchen table where they had always sat with Metz in the evening. It had been many months since they had discovered Thomas's old trunk filled with memories Metz had recorded. They had come to love the stories and had tied a ribbon around each bundle. What they had learned from their noble mother was the ways of love and integrity, great answers to great questions, the value and beauty of memory and friendship. They were overcome with the knowledge that they could and would carry on.

They had done all the right things to honor her. She was buried in the pretty Evergreen Cemetery, traditionally known as the African American cemetery. There was a small marble headstone, the kind that is flat to the ground and appropriately located next to her husband, Thomas. The cemetery is properly cared for by the townspeople and is the setting and burial ground for many former slaves and freed men and women. It was the right place for Metz to rest.

Tuney and Tick had saved the money to place a stone on her grave some time ago. On her stone was etched,

ELIZABETH "METZ" MACKEY
1919–2019
The lady who lived in The House on Fuller Street
"Here's to the people I have known, those
who gave grace and meaning to my life."

They acknowledged that even in death, she had made it about others, not herself. With full knowledge that they would revisit the memories many times, it was with gratitude and full hearts that, at least for that day, Tuney and Tick closed the lid of the trunk.

> "Losing someone is like when the sun comes through the window, moving across the room each hour, until night falls and all you do is try to remember the soothing shapes it made."
> —*Stewart Lewis*

Epilogue

Metz had many friends, and most of them were women. In some instances, she had male friends through her women friends and the church. But there were still fewer men.

Following trends, in Lexington there are more senior female African American women than there are senior African American men. That age cohort is a population that is living longer but aging in the extreme while many of the young have left to go where they can earn a more comfortable income. For various reasons, most of them troubling, the grandmothers have inherited the responsibility of raising many of these children. Most have experienced some great difficulties and most have turned to religion in the church for spiritual strength, social support systems, and a reason to keep trying.

There are many reasons to record these treasured stories, from the generation that most surely qualifies to be designated as Tom Brokaw's Greatest Generation. Metz has provided us with their unique narratives. Always remember what happened on Fuller Street. What an experience it was to have been there.

—Beverly Tucker, PhD

About the Author
Beverly Tucker, PhD

Beverly Tucker did her graduate studies at Texas Woman's University. After completing her doctorate in Social Psychology and a year of post-doctoral study in psychotherapy, she was appointed Clinical Director of the Medical Education and Research Foundation in Fort Worth, Texas. Dr. Tucker later established her own private practice. Having moved to Lexington—her husband's hometown—twenty two years ago, she now combines her interests in human behavior, historic preservation, and art. It is the interest in history and preservation that prompted her to accept a position on the Board of the Historic Lexington Foundation of which she has served as president both in the past and now in the present. Her interest in people was the impetus for her involvement in the oral history project. Dr. Tucker has provided the community with her dialogues with Diamond Hill and Green Hill, which includes the histories and her original art, some of which features portraits of those featured in the interviews.

Dr. Tucker is the author of *Blackberry Winter*, *The House on Fuller Street*, and *I'm not Alice, I'm Alice*. She lives in Lexington, Virginia, with her husband Dr. Spencer Tucker and her little dog, Sophie.

About the Illustrator
Bruce Macdonald

Bruce Macdonald created the portraits and cover art for this book—a fascinating story of African-Americans who comprise a valuable part of the rich history of Lexington, Virginia. This is the second collection of drawings Macdonald has created for the author and historian Beverly Tucker. Macdonald's artistic career began in Chicago, moved next to London where he illustrated for a number of leading authors and film makers of the mid 1960s. Finally he moved to New York and worked on various art or design assignments—before finally coming to the Shenandoah Valley in 2000.

www.ingramcontent.com/pod-product-compliance
Lightning Source LLC
Chambersburg PA
CBHW021018090426
42738CB00007B/820